Beyond Old MacDonald

Funny Poems from Down on the Farm

by **Charley Hoce**

Illustrated by **Eugenie Fernandes**

Wordsong
Boyds Mills Press

To Joanele for always believing and CJ for breakfast-bar critiques
—C. H.

For Isabelle Amelia Zeidner

—E. F.

Text copyright © 2005 by Charley Hoce
Illustrations © 2005 by Eugenie Fernandes
All rights reserved.

Wordsong
An Imprint of Boyds Mills Press, Inc.
A Highlights Company
815 Church Street
Honesdale, Pennsylvania 18431

Printed in China
www.boydsmillspress.com

Library of Congress Cataloging-in-Publication Data

Hoce, Charley E.
Beyond old MacDonald : funny poems from down on the farm / by Charley
Hoce ; illustrated by Eugenie Fernandes.
p. cm.
ISBN 1-59078-312-3 (alk. paper)
1. Farm life—Juvenile poetry. 2. Children's poetry, American.
I. Fernandes, Eugenie, 1943– II. Title.

PS3608.O26B49 2005
811'.6—dc22

2004010782

First edition, 2005

The text of this book is set in 16-point Usherwood Book.

10 9 8 7 6 5 4 3

Contents

WOOL-FREE

My Sheep Gave Me a Sweater

For a recent birthday gift
My sheep gave me a sweater.

I complimented their handiwork
But I should've known much better

For they didn't make a single yarn
Of the gift they'd given me.

It was mostly polyester
And totally wool free.

Mischievous Goat

The baby goat was scolded
For the mischievous things he did.
But no one got too angry
After all, he's just a kid.

6.

Chicken!

She's not afraid of fire
Or swarms of killer bees.
She swims in raging rivers
To rid herself of fleas.

She attacks F-5 tornados
And pecks them in the eye.
She jumps without a parachute
From high up in the sky.

She takes on the meanest bully
Even if she takes a lickin'.
My chicken may be many things
But she surely isn't chicken.

Holey Cow!

When people see my holey cow
They have to stop and stare.
For when she takes a tiny step
Milk leaks everywhere.

My Pig Will Dance

My pig will dance at parties
She'll sing at local proms.
She'll do a double backflip
And cheer with her pom-poms.

She likes to tell disgusting jokes
To people on the street
Then stand upon her piggy head
And play drums with her feet.

She's ornery and rambunctious—
Not at all like Mary's lamb.
If you haven't guessed already
My pig is quite a ham.

Counting Sheep

I've always heard of counting sheep
But I don't think it's true.
My sheep can only baah and bleat
And can't count more than two.

Milkshake

I made a milkshake while at the farm.
No one was hurt; I caused no harm.
But the angry farmer raised his brow
Because I shook his favorite cow.

True Love

The tractor loved the wagon
That she saw out in the field.

The farmer tried to intervene
But her love refused to yield.

She finally met her true love
In a field out by the ditch.

And before anyone could stop them
They were happily hitched.

The Horses' Union

The horses started a union
To demand more oats and hay.
But they never passed the motion
Since they always voted, "Neigh!"

Our Hog Is Not a Pig

Our hog has a great appetite
For foods of many kinds.

He loves fresh fruit and vegetables
But please remove the rind.

He likes to sip his bowl of soup
With just the right-size spoon.

He has to have his cup of tea
With his meal at noon.

He will not eat a salad
Without the dressing on the side.

He refuses to eat any food
If it has been deep-fried.

He's always counting calories
When he's out to eat.

He puts the napkin on his lap
In case he isn't neat.

Our hog is very mannerly
Although he's round and big.

We're all extremely proud of him
Since he is not a pig.

Our Goat Will Eat Most Anything

Our goat will eat most anything
His stomach will fit in
But one thing that he never eats
Is sticks of margarine.

It isn't that it tastes bad
Or makes his stomach flutter.
It's just that it won't help him
To be a better butt-er.

Farm Family

My mother patches all my jeans
My grandma makes my clothes
But when he's on a tractor
My dad's the one who sows.

When My Cow Goes Dancing

When my cow goes dancing
At the weekly fashion ball,
She always wears a muumuu
Since it makes her calves look small.

My Rhododendron's Yawning

My rhododendron's yawning,
My rose needs tucking in.
My tulip wants his teddy bear
To hold beneath his chin.

My marigold would like a drink,
My fern a story read.
The time has come to put my plants
Into their flowerbed.

My Horse He Cannot Whinny

My horse he cannot whinny,
My horse he cannot neigh.
My horse has caught a nasty cold,
My horse is hoarse today.

Bum Steer

He drove in a ditch this morning.
He grazed a tree last week.
Whenever I drive with him
I just don't dare to peek.

I'm not sure he'll pass his driver's test
With the way he weaves and veers—
But he'll never drive my car or truck
Because my steer can't steer.

Swan Singer

Our swan sings songs that are short
Our swan sings songs that are long
Tomorrow she's leaving for Hollywood
Come listen to her swan song.

Goose Down Pillow

I've always heard a pillow
Filled with soft goose down
Was the very best way
To get to Sleepy Town.

I'm not sure I agree with that
Or maybe mine's a fake.
I just know her honking
Keeps me wide-awake.

Bullish Behavior

We took our bull to a china shop
To enjoy a shopping spree.
The owner seemed unhappy
And eyed us suspiciously.

But our bull was very careful
As he wandered through the aisles.
In fact he moved quite smoothly
With agility and guile.

Everyone is happy
Since he didn't break a thing
And he makes a fashion statement
With his porcelain nose ring.

A Shocking Development

Sometimes my brother has no sense—
Like when he jumped the electric fence.
He thought he was a track star jock.
When he learned he wasn't—it was a shock!

Barnyard Rooster

Never a feather out of place
Even when rising from bed.
It must be very handy
To have a comb upon your head.

Ants in My . . .

My lettuce jiggles in the breeze.
My turnips quiver with my peas.
My tomato plants they scratch and squirm.
My lima beans are wiggle worms.
My red-hot peppers twist and dance—
I think I have ants in my plants.

Dirty Pumpkins

Our truck was filled with pumpkins
That needed to be washed.
We drove them down a bumpy road
Now all we have is squash.

From the Diary of an Escaped Sheep

I went under the fence this morning.
No one knows where I am.
I love the freedom that I've found.
I'm a sheep that's on the lam.

Her Ponytail

Her ponytail looks very soft
Her ponytail is long.

I want to pull her ponytail
Although I know it's wrong

So slowly, slowly, slowly
I extend my trembling hand

And grab her lovely ponytail
Up by the rubber band.

I give her ponytail a tug . . .
Now I'm flying through the air.

I'll never again pull a ponytail
When I'm at the County Fair.

25

Wild and Woolly

Shearing their wool in a Mohawk,
Bungeeing off of the barn,
Scaling Manure Mountain,
Dirt-biking all over the farm,

Hang-gliding off of the silo,
Rapelling down a ravine,
Skateboarding in the pasture,
Flipping on trampolines.

Joy-riding on a tractor,
Skiing down Avalanche Hill,
Are just some things my flock does
When they're looking for sheep thrills.

Unconscious Goose

Our goose was knocked unconscious
When he was hit with a hockey puck.
Everyone tried to warn him
But he ignored our shouts of "Duck!"

Quit Horsing Around

"Quit horsing around!" is all I hear;
It makes me want to revolt.
I'm not sure what they expect of me,
After all, I am a colt!

A Pig Tale

Curlers are not necessary
To groom my favorite pig.
She never needs a permanent
Or a fashion wig.

The reason is quite simple;
She never, ever fails
To rise and shine each morning
With a naturally curly tail.

Dinnertime

Sitting round the dinner table
Looking at the food:

The bread Mom baked with loving care
The tomatoes that she stewed.

There's heaps of creamy butter
That Papa churned this morn.

And Grandma spent an hour or two
Husking all the corn.

I helped pick the lima beans
And free them from their shells.

The food all looks delicious
And it has a luscious smell.

Everybody pitches in
When we have a meal to make.

And we always save the best for last
Strawberry CHORE-cake!

Wordplay Guide

When I wrote this collection, my goal was to make children laugh and become aware that words and how we use them can be down-right funny. So share all thirty poems with children and enjoy the barnyard-based wordplay—and with the following eighteen poems, point out the language skills I've listed, if you wish.